Understanding
LEBANON
Today

LEBANON

Laura Perdew

Mitchell Lane
PUBLISHERS
P.O. Box 196
Hockessin, Delaware 19707

A Kid's Guide to
THE MIDDLE EAST

Tall Kalakh

Al Qubayyat

Halba

Al Mina • Tripoli

Ash Shamal

Al Hirmil

Shikka

Al Qa'

Amyun

Al Batrun

Bsharri

Duma

Jubayl

Lebanon

AL Biqa

Jabal Lubnan

Juniyah

(Bekka Valley)

Ba'labekk

Beirut

Bkfayya

Bayrut

B'abda

Zahlah

Rayaq

Alayh

Shtawrah

Ad Damur

Bayt ad Din

Barja

Al Bliqa

Jubb Jennin

Sidon

Jazzin

Al Qir'awn

Az Zahrani

Rashayya

As Sarafand

An Nabatiyah Nt Tahta

Marjiyun

Tyre

Al Janub

An Naqurah

Bint Jubayl

Rumaysh

TURKEY

SYRIA

LEBANON IRAQ AFGHANISTAN

PALESTINE IRAN

ISRAEL JORDAN

SAUDI
ARABIA

Mitchell Lane
PUBLISHERS

Printing   1   2   3   4   5   6   7   8   9

Library of Congress Cataloging-in-Publication Data
Perdew, Laura.
 Understanding Lebanon today / by Laura Perdew.
     pages cm. — (A kid's guide to the Middle East)
 Includes bibliographical references and index.
 ISBN 978-1-61228-653-2 (library bound)
 1. Lebanon—Juvenile literature. I. Title.
 DS80.P47 2015
 956.92—dc23
                                                                      2014008837

eBook ISBN: 9781612286761

PUBLISHER'S NOTE: The narrative used in portions of this book are an aid to comprehension. This narrative is based on the author's extensive research as to what actually occurs in a child's life in Lebanon. It is subject to interpretation and might not be indicative of every child's life in Lebanon. It is representative of some children and is based on research the author believes to be accurate. Documentation of such research is contained on pp. 60–61.

The Internet sites referenced herein were active as of the publication date. Due to the fleeting nature of some web sites, we cannot guarantee they will all be active when you are reading this book.

To reflect current usage, we have chosen to use the secular era designations BCE ("before the common era") and CE ("of the common era") instead of the traditional designations BC ("before Christ") and AD (*anno Domini,* "in the year of the Lord").

PBP

CONTENTS

BOLD words in text can be found in the glossary

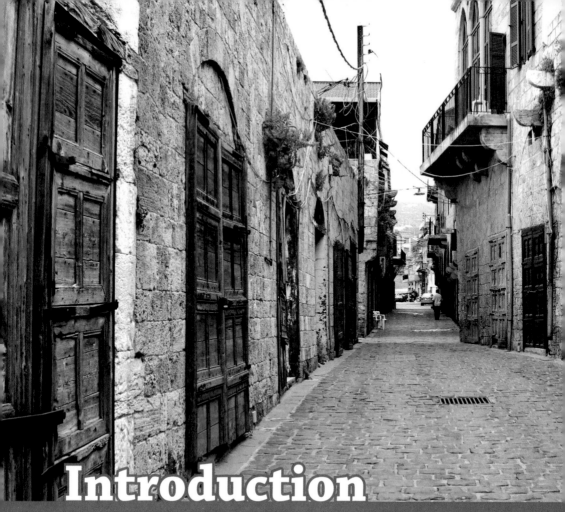

Introduction

Lebanon is a small, vibrant nation at the western edge of the Mediterranean Sea. It is bordered by Israel and Syria.[1] It sits at the heart of the Middle East, where East meets West. Because of its location, Lebanon has been at the center of trade since the time of the **Phoenicians**. The Phoenicians developed sea trade routes across the Mediterranean. Later they sailed as far as Europe and Western Asia. They traded goods, but also ideas and culture. This legacy has helped shape Lebanon.

Lebanon today remains highly invested in trade and open to ideas and cultures from around the world. It is a modern nation, with its cultural roots firmly in the past, yet it is also a nation divided. The country gained its independence in 1943. At that time, Christians and **Muslims** were at odds. The disputes

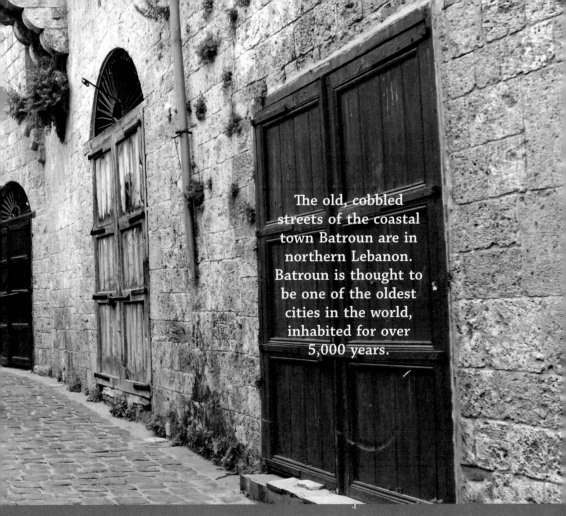

The old, cobbled streets of the coastal town Batroun are in northern Lebanon. Batroun is thought to be one of the oldest cities in the world, inhabited for over 5,000 years.

between these groups led to a brutal civil war. It lasted fifteen years. Since it ended in 1989, the country has rebuilt. Now, Lebanon is divided by two different Muslim sects. This division is also political. The different sects cannot agree on how to run the country. Some government officials want to maintain long-standing ties with the West. Others do not. They disagree on how to deal with their neighbors, Syria and Israel. Some are forward-thinking. Others are more rooted in the past. These differences continue to result in violence across Lebanon.

But above all the people of Lebanon are resilient. They are proud and determined. They look to the future, optimistic that Lebanon as a nation will prevail once again.

A Lebanese teacher lectures her all-boy class. In some schools boys and girls are separated, but in others students are mixed.

CHAPTER 1
Living in Lebanon

Twelve-year old Imad wakes early on a school day. When he turns on the water for a shower, he is grateful that it comes on. As he showers, the water slows to a trickle. Imad hurries. He pulls on a pair of jeans, then looks for a clean school shirt. When he can't find what he's looking for, he looks through his older brother's clothes. Surely his brother will have a clean uniform shirt Imad can borrow. His brother won't mind—they share just about everything. Before going to the kitchen, Imad takes a moment to tidy up the bathroom as he does every day.

By the time he gets to the kitchen, his father has left for work. Imad's mother sighs. "We are almost out of water. Again," she says. His mother is upset because she will have to take off work. She must call the water truck. She will also have to wait for it. It may take an hour for the truck to come. It may take the day. It is not uncommon that the system is without water. Families have to rely on trucks to deliver water to storage tanks. Imad feels a little guilty for taking a shower, even though he was quick. Still, he knows the water would have run out anyway.[1]

Imad's mother gives her boys money to buy breakfast on the way to school. Imad says goodbye to his mother and looks her in the eye to show his respect for her. His brother follows. When Imad and his brother leave their Beirut apartment building, others are waiting. The kids are neighborhood friends and cousins. They have known the other kids their whole lives. Even the friends that are not family are extremely close. They all look out for one another and will probably do so into the future. In fact, one of Imad's closest friends is the son of his father's boyhood friend. They live just below them in the apartment building.

On the walk to school, Imad stops at his favorite vendor. The man serves **manouché** (man-OU-shay), an **Arab**-style bread. First the man spreads a paste on the flat, round bread. The paste includes **zaatar** (ZA-tar), a blend of spices and sesame seeds, mixed with olive oil. Next the vendor adds yogurt, tomatoes, olives and mint. When he is finished, he rolls the bread with the ingredients inside. Imad and his brother eat as they continue to school.[2]

Schoolchildren share a breakfast of manouché, a Lebanese flatbread flavored with a paste of spices and olive oil.

When they reach the public secondary school, the kids scatter to their classrooms. Imad and the other students, both boys and girls, stay in the same room all day. Different teachers come in to teach different subjects. Imad works hard in school. He is from a respectable family, with a respectable name. Imad knows he must make them proud. Plus, he will need the education to get a good job to earn a living for his own family someday. One of Imad's favorite times of the day is when he is allowed to use the computer. He likes to look up places all over the world. He hopes to travel the world someday. Imad also has an American friend he's been exchanging emails with since he was in elementary school.

After school Imad walks home with the same group of kids. They drop their bags at home. Then they meet in the park like they do almost every day. One of Imad's cousins has a basketball. It is old and scuffed, but it holds enough air they can play a game with it. There is no permanent basketball hoop in the park. But today, one of Imad's cousins finds an old bike tire rim lying on the ground. "Our lucky day!" he exclaims, holding the rim above his head. "A new hoop!" The boys spend almost a half hour fixing the rim to a board. It is not regulation, but it is the best they've had in a while. The boys play a friendly game. The girls stand along the sidelines talking.[3]

At dinner time, Imad and his brother go back to their apartment. Both parents are home. His father is reading the newspaper. His mom is cooking dinner. For dinner she prepares

IN CASE YOU WERE WONDERING

Do people get frustrated that the power and water go out?
Yes! People are extremely frustrated. But they've done something about it. In many places people have created businesses providing generators for power and bringing water to storage tanks by truck.[4]

kibbeh

an array of food. On the table are olives, hummus, stuffed tomatoes, fresh fruit and a salad. She has also prepared baked **kibbeh** (KI-beh). Kibbeh is a favorite food in Lebanon. It is made from lamb ground into a paste. Then it is mixed with many spices and baked.[5]

During dinner Imad's father talks about the latest conflicts on the Syrian border. Problems between religious groups have gotten worse. The violence has spread into Lebanon. Imad feels his parents' worry. For all of them it is constant. Imad and his brother have known no other Lebanon. Throughout their lifetimes, attacks and bombings on the country have been a constant threat. Luckily, the fighting has not come to their neighborhood. Still, there is evidence all around them of the violence of the civil war. It scares Imad. He is happy when his mother changes the subject to the family gathering on Sunday. Every week the whole family gathers at his grandfather's apartment after church. Being with family makes Imad feel safe and strong. They will eat and talk for hours. The talk is frequently about what is going on in their country. Yet it is always filled with hope. Things are changing. Imad feels the responsibility to keep that going for his family, and for his country. Imad knows he is part of a new generation.[6]

IN CASE YOU WERE WONDERING

Why is there a tree on Lebanon's flag?
The tree in the center of the flag is a cedar tree. The Lebanese believe that the trees were planted by God. They have been an important resource in Lebanon since the time of the Phoenicians, and are now protected.[7]

LEBANON'S GEOGRAPHY

Lebanon is a small country no bigger than the state of Connecticut. It has four distinct geographic regions. First is the coastline of Lebanon. It borders the Mediterranean Sea. The weather there is temperate. Summers are hot and sunny while winters are cool and rainy. There are numerous coastal cities, including the capital, Beirut. People in the region enjoy the beaches, and even snorkeling among ancient Phoenician ruins!

Next, bordering the coastal plain to the east is the Mount Lebanon Range. Among these mountains is the country's highest peak, which is 10,130 feet high. There is snow in the winter and people can ski there. In the summer there are trails to hike on. The Mount Lebanon Range is home to the nation's Cedar Reserves. The country once had abundant cedar forests. Over time, resources were depleted due to the over-use of cedar for construction and trade. The remaining cedar forests are now protected. The tree is the Lebanese national symbol.

The Afqa Cave, waterfall, and spring are a geological wonder in Lebanon's mountains.

The central valley in Lebanon is the agricultural center. The Békaa Valley is a high plateau, with mountain ranges on both sides and rivers running through it. It was known in ancient times as "the breadbasket" of the Roman Empire. Today many crops are grown there, including olives, grapes, potatoes and wheat.

The fourth region of Lebanon is the Anti-Lebanon Range. These arid mountains form Lebanon's border with Syria.[8]

Lebanon has fifteen rivers, too. Each one of them begins in Lebanon's own mountains.[9]

Sidon's Sea Castle is one of the most prominent archaeological sites in Sidon, Lebanon. The city of Sidon is found on the Mediterranean coast of Lebanon. This ancient Phoenician city has been of great religious, political, and commercial value; it is believed to have been inhabited since 4000 BC. During the 13th century, the Crusaders built Sidon's Sea Castle as a fortress on a small island connected to the mainland by a narrow roadway. In time past, the island was the site of a temple to Melqart, a Phoenician god.

CHAPTER 2
History

Lebanon's history is one of prosperity and ruin, invasion and independence, turmoil and peace. It is also one of resilience.

The first inhabitants of Lebanon arrived there millions of years ago. Ancient tools have been discovered in the region. They show that the people were hunters and fishermen. Some of the first villages were established around 7500 BC. At that time people began farming. They **domesticated** animals and made pottery.

The first civilization in Lebanon was Phoenician. It began around 3,500 BC. The Phoenicians were excellent fishermen, seamen and traders. They built many coastal cities. Their skills allowed the Phoenicians to dominate trade in the Mediterranean for hundreds of years. They traded cedar, olive oil and wine to Egypt. In exchange, they brought back metal and ivory. Later they set up routes to trade with Europe and Western Asia. Their trade also brought foreign ideas, cultures, religions, and new political concepts into Lebanon. For this reason, it is often considered the "Cradle of Civilization."[1]

For hundreds of years the Phoenicians enjoyed success and self-rule. During this prosperity, the Phoenicians created textiles and carved ivory. They were skilled at metal working and glass blowing, too. The alphabet as it is known today originated with the Phoenicians.[2]

Following that, though, were centuries of invasion and domination. In fact, the entire Middle East region experienced this turmoil. Lebanon and the surrounding areas were controlled by Assyrians, Babylonians, Persians, Greeks, Romans, and

Ottomans. At the end of World War I, Lebanon was under French control. At last, in 1943, Lebanon became an independent country.[4]

Government

Today Lebanon is a **democracy**. It operates on a **parliamentary system** of government. The parliament is called the National Assembly. The 128 members of the assembly are elected by the people. The National Assembly elects the president. The President selects the prime minister, who heads the National Assembly. The executive, judicial and legislative branches of the government are separate.[5]

When Lebanon's constitution was written, it distributed government jobs and offices between the different religious groups. The goal was to keep a peaceful balance. It would also prevent any one **sect** from having too much power. The president was to be a Maronite Christian. The prime minister would be a Sunni Muslim. The Speaker of the National Assembly was to be a Shiite Muslim.

Muslims thought the division of power was unequal. The division was based on the number of Muslims and Christians living in the country. But the numbers came from an old census. Muslims believed there were more Muslims than the census showed. Thus, they felt they did not get their fair share of power. In part, this was the root of religious tensions in the new Republic of Lebanon.[6]

Modern Lebanon

Following WWII, the country of Israel was formed. Because of this, refugees from Palestine began to flood into Lebanon in the late 1940s. They were Muslims seeking refuge from the new Jewish nation. Then the Palestinian Liberation Organization began to use the refugee camps as a base. The PLO wanted an independent Palestinian state. They wanted to destroy the new Israel. Most Lebanese did not want to be involved in the clash between Israel and Palestine. They didn't even want the PLO in their country. However, the PLO group launched attacks against Israel from Lebanon. Refugees continued to flood into the country.[7]

At the same time, the long-standing rivalry between Christians and Muslims simmered. It evolved into a civil war that began in 1975. Syria sent troops into Lebanon in 1976. They stayed for almost thirty years. Meanwhile, Israel took over the southern part of Lebanon. Thus the Palestinians, Syria and Israel were all fighting their own wars, using Lebanon as the battleground. Christians and Muslims were in constant battle as well. Peace keeping forces were sent to Lebanon in 1982, including US Marines. But in 1983, suicide bombers attacked the Marine barracks and the US Embassy. The US withdrew forces in 1984 because of the excessive violence.[8]

Finally, on October 22, 1989, the Ta'if Agreements were signed. The agreements ended the civil war. Muslims and Christians were given equal power in the government. It also called for strengthening Lebanon's armed forces. Foreign troops were expected to withdraw.[9]

Tens of thousands of people had died. The country was still occupied by foreigners who did not leave. Israel had troops in the south. Syria controlled politics and economics in Lebanon. The cities were in ruin.

At last, in the late 1990s, Lebanon began to recover. The man leading the change was the nation's Prime Minister, Rafik Hariri. He had been elected in 1992. Hariri had a vision of a vibrant, independent nation. With his ideas put into action, Lebanon's economy was thriving by the early 2000s. Yet the country was still controlled by Syria. For a time, Hariri accepted this. The Syrians helped maintain peace. Then, when Israel finally withdrew from Lebanon in 2000, the government wanted Syria to withdraw as well. Syria did not.

On February 14, 2005, Hariri was killed in a truck bomb. Twenty-two others died, too. At first, the attack was blamed on Syria. Protests broke out. Lebanon again demanded that Syria withdraw. At last, after 30 years, Syrian troops left Lebanon.[10]

Modern Lebanon remains at a crossroads between war and peace. The **sectarian** tensions continue to divide the country. It causes violence. Each group wants its people to lead the country. No one seems to want to compromise. It also keeps the country from moving forward. In addition, border conflicts with both Israel and Syria erupt continually. And the country itself sits at the center of strife between competing groups in the Middle East.[11]

The grave site of slain Prime Minister Rafik Hariri in downtown Beirut

FAMOUS SITES AND LANDMARKS IN LEBANON

The many different civilizations that have invaded Lebanon have left their mark. For example, the Byblos Ruins date back to the time of the Phoenicians. The town was a major port in the Mediterranean. Since then, other civilizations have added to it. It is the oldest inhabited city in the world. There are temples built by the Phoenicians and a theatre built by the Romans. The Crusaders also built a castle there.[12]

When the Muslims entered the Békaa Valley they built the town of Anjar around 700 CE. It is still there today. The remains of the city's walls, streets, public bathhouses, and more are still visible.[13]

The Romans built numerous temples when they controlled the region. In the town of Tyre there are many Roman ruins still standing. One is a hippodrome, or stadium. The Romans used to have chariot races there in front of crowds of up to 20,000. But the best Roman ruins are in Baalbeck. The Romans built their largest temples outside of Rome there. It took over 10,000 slaves more than 200 years to build. Much of their work is well-preserved. Visitors can visit the temple center and stare up at the ancient columns. They can also stand at sacrificial sites or admire stone statues.[14]

During the reign of the Ottoman Empire, the Beiteddine Palace was built. It is an extravagant palace on the top of a mountain with courtyards, mosaics and fountains. It overlooks the Békaa Valley. A festival is held there every summer.[15]

In Tripoli there are numerous ancient sites. There are medieval mosques and a Muslim school. Castles built by the Crusaders still stand. Non-religious buildings include bath houses and **souks**, or open markets.[16]

The Beiteddine Palace was built in the 19th century and sits 900 meters (2,953 feet) above sea level.

In Beirut, Lebanon, worshippers fill the inside courtyard of the Armenian Catholic Church during Palm Sunday Mass. When the church is full, people also gather in the courtyard to listen to Mass through speakers.

CHAPTER 3
Cultures

Today more than four million people live in Lebanon. Of these people, eighty-five percent are Lebanese. There are also more than 400,000 Palestinians. Many of these are **refugees**. There are Syrian refugees living in Lebanon as well. People from other countries live in Lebanon to work, too.[1]

Most people living in Lebanon, even those from other countries, are Arab. Arabs make up ninety-five percent of the population. "Arab" refers to those who are descendants of people from the Arabian Peninsula and northern Africa. As a result, Lebanon has an Arab culture. Yet young people in Lebanon worry about what being Arab means in the modern world. Many people think of terrorists when someone says "Arab." Others imagine people riding camels in the desert. Young people in Lebanon do not want to be thought of in these terms. They embrace their Arab roots. But they simply want to be referred to as "Lebanese."

All Lebanese are sociable, generous, **entrepreneurial** people. They are survivors. They have overcome centuries of conquest and internal conflict. Lebanese people are proud of their heritage. Yet despite these commonalities, the people of Lebanon are strongly divided by religion.

When Lebanon was part of the Roman Empire, Christianity was the official religion. Then **Islam** emerged in the 7th century. Followers are called **Muslims**. Muslims spread their religion in the Mediterranean region. They conquered new areas of the Middle East. They forced non-Muslims to convert. Christians who refused to convert fled to Lebanon's mountains. The

Crusades began in 1095. It was an effort by Christians to recapture their land and to save sacred sites that were ravaged by Muslims. They were driven out of Lebanon in the late 13th century,[2] yet the discord between Christians and Muslims remained.

Christians

The Middle East is where Christianity began. Lebanon itself is mentioned in the Bible dozens of times. Lebanon's famed cedars are even in the Bible as symbols of strength and beauty. Many ancient Biblical sites can still be found there today.

Facing strong religious persecution in the 10th century, the Maronite Christians took refuge in the mountains of Lebanon. There they found shelter and organized their church. In the 1700s, the Maronite church joined the Catholic Church. However, Maronites maintain their own practices and traditions.[3]

In modern Lebanon, thirty-nine percent are Christian. This includes Greek Orthodox, Maronites, other Catholics, and Protestants.[4] Lebanon is the only country in the Middle East where Christians maintain some political power, but Christians are worried that their numbers are declining. This is partly due to low birth rates and emigration. With fewer Christians being born and more Christians leaving, their influence and power in Lebanon may be weakening.

Muslims

While the Middle East is the birthplace of Christianity, the majority of people living in Lebanon today, sixty percent, are Muslim. The two main sects of Muslims are the Shiites and the Sunni. There are also several smaller sects living in Lebanon.[5] A sect is a small part of a larger religion. They share some beliefs, yet disagree on some basic ideas of the main group.

The division between the two main sects began over who should be the heir to the religion's founder, Muhammad. The Sunnis believed that Muhammad did not name a successor. Therefore, the strongest of the religion's followers should become the Muslim leader. On the other hand, the Shiites wanted only Muhammad's ancestors to be leaders. This created a clear split within the Islamic world that still exists.

Following a battle in the late 7th century, the Sunnis became the controlling sect. For the most part, Sunnis have dominated the region ever since. The Shiites remained a powerful, but divided, minority. Among Shiites there was another dispute over which descendants had the right to rule Islam. The Druze and Allawis sects emerged because of this. Some Muslims believe that these sects are not true followers of Islam.[6]

Hezbollah

Hezbollah is a militant group of Shiite Muslims. It was founded in 1982 when Israel invaded Lebanon. The Hezbollah (which means "Party of God") does not believe that Israel should even be a country. They are also largely anti-American. In fact, they are against any Western involvement in the Middle East. The group is supported by both Syria and Iran.

Many people believe that Hezbollah is simply a terrorist organization. Backed by Iran, they have access to state-of-the-

IN CASE YOU WERE WONDERING

Do Christians, Shiites and Sunnis live near each other, or is everything divided?

In many places in Lebanon they do live near each other and there is not a problem. People from different sects can be neighbors and friends. Sometimes people even marry someone from a different sect.

art weapons. In 1997, the United States labeled Hezbollah as a terrorist threat. On the other hand, the group defines itself as a Lebanese resistance movement. Members of Hezbollah say they are simply protecting their country.

Hezbollah's power continues to grow in Lebanon. It has even evolved into a political party. Since the early 1990s, the group has gained more parliamentary seats in national elections. The group has built schools and a modern hospital. It runs TV and radio stations and even maintains a website.[7,8]

Palestinians

The country of Israel was formed in 1948. It gave Jews a home in the Palestine region. Immediately there was conflict between Palestinian Arabs and Palestinian Jews.[9] As a result, many Palestinian Arabs fled to **refugee** camps in nearby countries. There are twelve camps still in Lebanon. The camps are cramped. Conditions are poor. One such place, Shatila, was built in 1949. Generations of children have been raised in the camp that was never meant to be permanent. It is one square kilometer in size, and is home to 12,000 people.[10]

Palestinians make up about ten percent of Lebanon's population.[11] But they are not citizens. They do not have many rights in Lebanon. They cannot vote and finding jobs is very difficult.[12]

IN CASE YOU WERE WONDERING
Do kids go to school in the Palestinian refugee camps?
Schools have been built in the camps, and kids go to school there much like in the rest of the world. They study religion, Arabic, and other subjects. Children are happy to go to school because there is not much to do on the crowded streets.[13]

PERSPECTIVE

Everything in Lebanon is a matter of perspective. Each person's perspective, or viewpoint, depends on their religion and their family's values. Yet these different perspectives make it difficult to move Lebanon forward in a positive way.

Imagine that you and several classmates have been given a ball. You are all standing in an outlined field. Together you must make up a game to play. You need rules. You need to decide who's in charge. Yet no one agrees.

You and a friend have one idea. Maybe you want create a game sort of like soccer. But two other classmates want to play something more like capture the flag. Others make suggestions. At some point you realize that you have three separate groups of kids. Each group has a different idea. All of you try to come up with a plan to decide who's in charge of the game. Each group gets a representative, chosen by the others. You still cannot decide on what to play. No one wants to compromise. All you can agree on is that you have a ball, a field, and three teams.

This is sort of what it is like in Lebanon. While all Lebanese are proud of their heritage, few can agree on how to run the country. Each religion, and even the sects within the religions, have a different perspective. How they believe the country should be run differs because of their beliefs. Because of this, the government is very weak. It is also unstable. All of these different groups cannot find a way to get along and this leads to fighting.

Lebanese citizens protest a 2012 bombing in Beirut by Israel as border tensions increase.

Syrian refugee children go to collect drinking water in Anjar, Lebanon since there is no running water in the camps.

CHAPTER 4
Current Issues

In Lebanon today, peace and stability are fragile. Many Lebanese believe it is the government's fault. It is full of corruption. Lebanon is supposed to be a democracy. However, officials in the National Assembly pass down their seat to children and friends. Thus alliances always stay the same. As a result, progress can't be made. It is like a permanent stalemate. And no one is willing to negotiate or compromise.[1] In fact, in 2013, the government was barely functioning. Many cabinet members had stepped down. The different factions could not come to any agreements. This left the Lebanese government completely ineffective. It left Lebanon vulnerable.

Further, Lebanese people are frustrated that their government does not focus on helping the people. While politicians are wealthy, most Lebanese are not. People struggle to earn a living. Wages are low. Further, the services to people are unreliable. Streets flood because they are not maintained. Power outages occur regularly. Water is available only a few hours a day. Citizens feel the government should do more to improve the **infrastructure** for everyone.[2]

Drinking Water
In Lebanon, most people only have access to water for a few hours a day. And the water that does come out of the tap is often not fit for drinking. Lebanese who have some money buy bottled water. Others pay water trucks to fill storage tanks. This has been an ongoing problem. The government is currently working on the issue. In the past, water projects have included

building dams. Some of these even provide hydroelectric power in addition to water storage. Water laws have also been passed. Strategic plans have been put in place, yet the number one concern in Lebanon now is the safety of the water. The Lebanese are hoping their government will now put the plan into action.[3]

Sectarian Tensions

Following the civil war, Shiite and Sunni Muslims and Christians were each given political power. And for a time, there were no major problems. Yet Lebanon is like a simmering pot on the stove. In 2013, the heat was turned up. Sectarian violence broke out again. This time the fighting was between the Sunni and Shiite Muslims. Car bomb attacks became common. Sunni mosques were targeted. Even the cities of Beirut and Tripoli experienced the new wave of violence. Dozens died.

The rivalry between religious groups is also to blame for many political assassinations. No one is ever held accountable. In late 2013, another politician was killed by a car bomb. Mohammed Chatah was a Sunni aligned with Western allies. He spoke against Syria's president, Bashar al-Assad. He worked against

Mohammed Chatah had good relations with the US. Though no one was ever found responsible for his death, it is believed he was targeted because he was outspoken against Hezbollah and the Syrian president, Assad.

the Shiite Hezbollah. The bombing occurred in the business district of Beirut.[4]

Many in Beirut were worried. They feared for their safety, as they did during the civil war. They were also concerned that Lebanon was headed toward civil war again. Others warned that the conflicts in Lebanon were the same ones occurring all over the Middle East. Across the region, Sunni Muslims were supported by Saudi Arabia. The Shiites and Hezbollah were supported by Iran. The wars between these groups began in Iraq and Syria then spilled into Lebanon. The conflicts threatened to destroy the region.[5]

Syrian Conflict

The war in Syria made the tension in Lebanon worse. The Lebanese Hezbollah supported the Syrian president, Assad. His regime was made up of Shiite Muslims. They fought the Sunni rebels. This incited more violence between Sunni and Shiite Muslims in Lebanon. Both Sunni and Shiite villages experienced regular rocket attacks.

Many in Lebanon want their country to stay neutral. Yet Hezbollah's involvement dragged Lebanon into the conflict. There were many consequences for Lebanon. First, it endangered Lebanon's fragile government. It put at risk the precarious balance the different sects had achieved. Next, the war affected the economy in the Hezbollah dominated regions. Tourists

IN CASE YOU WERE WONDERING

What are the Syrian refugee camps like?
Most people in the camps live in tents with their whole family. They do not have running water, nor do they have heat, which is a great concern during the harsh winters in Lebanon's mountains.

stopped visiting the ancient Roman ruins there because it was too dangerous. Eateries and shops were empty. Trade between the two countries also halted. Tourism in Beirut and the rest of Lebanon is likely to slow down or stop as well. To make things even more complicated, more than one million Syrian refugees fled into Lebanon. They compete with Lebanese for jobs and housing.

Finally, the refugees (mostly Sunni) increased the imbalance in Lebanon between Christians and Muslims. Some Christians are worried that they will eventually be driven out of Lebanon.[6]

Emigration

Lebanon has a rich history of being adventurous travelers. This has resulted in new ideas and cultures being brought back to Lebanon. It is these forces that helped Lebanon become what it is today. Unfortunately, nowadays, more of Lebanon's citizens are leaving the country and not returning. Estimates are that ten million Lebanese live outside of Lebanon.[7]

This is true for people of all sects. People are tired of the corruption in the government. Jobs are scarce. And they are tired of living in a country where nothing ever seems to change or move forward. While proud of being Lebanese, many feel the need to leave their country to move on with their own lives.[8]

Lebanon's location in the Middle East and its heritage puts it in a unique position. For thousands of years Lebanese have navigated the world. They have brought back with them goods, services and ideas. The country has become a center for banking. All of this has made Lebanon one of the most progressive cities in the Arab World. Yet its geographic position also puts it at a crossroads. It is where East meets West. It is at the center of thousands of years of turmoil.[9]

TRIAL FOR THE
RAFIK HARIRI ASSASSINATION

In 2005, the Lebanese Prime Minister Rafik Hariri was assassinated. He was killed by a truck bomb that also took the lives of 22 others. Hariri was a Sunni. He was also a wealthy businessman with dreams of a new Lebanon. He wanted to rebuild his country and return it to the prosperous and peaceful days it enjoyed before the civil war.

After Hariri's death, no one was held responsible. Finally, in early 2014, four Hezbollah members were on trial for Hariri's murder. The trial was held outside of Lebanon. Those who heard the case were a special group put together by the United Nations. The trial was held without the four suspects. Hezbollah leaders refused to turn them over.

Many Lebanese are glad to see the trial happening at all. In a time when groups act without consequences, some hope the trial will bring justice. A member of Hariri's political party said, "To Lebanese people [the trial] means the dream of Rafik Hariri to build Lebanon, the country of constitution, the country of freedom, the country of coexistence. The start of this tribunal is a dream and it's a historic moment for all the Lebanese people. We have been attacked as politicians in Lebanon for years. It is not only the assassination of former Prime Minister Rafik Hariri. We have had so many assassinations for tens of years and we now believe this will be the first time we reach justice."

Hezbollah, however, believes that the trial is a conspiracy. They believe it is all a scheme against Hezbollah by the United States and Israel.[10]

Statue of Rafik Hariri in Beirut, Lebanon, at the site where he was assassinated.

A Lebanese family is shown wearing Western-style clothing; yet because of this family's Muslim beliefs, the mother has her hair and ears covered also.

CHAPTER 5
Family

Family is extremely important to the Lebanese people. Families usually live very close to each other. Aunts, uncles, cousins and grandparents often live in the same building. Sometimes they even live right next door! They all take care of one another. Whenever someone is sick or in trouble, the family is always there to help. Family members assist each other with money matters. Elderly are cared for by the family. There are no nursing homes in Lebanon because the families take care of their people.

In urban families, both parents usually have a job. This is because it is difficult to earn a living in Lebanon. At home, the mother is still responsible for the housework and children. The father is the head of the household. He must approve all major family decisions.

Children usually live at home until they are married. In Lebanon wages are low and real estate is expensive. Men often wait until they are almost 30 years old to marry because they want to have a stable job. Sometimes, a newly married couple will move in with the groom's parents. They do this so they can save money to buy a home of their own.

Every Sunday the whole family gathers. They all meet at the **patriarch's** home for Sunday lunch. The patriarch is the oldest living male relative. This might be a grandfather or uncle or cousin. This is the way for all families in Lebanon, no matter the religion. Because of this, everything shuts down on Sundays.[4]

Food

Food in Lebanon has many influences. Phoenicians, Romans, Arabs, Crusaders, Ottomans, and French have all shaped Lebanese cuisine. Plus, since Lebanon has been at the center of trading on the Mediterranean, cooks utilize a variety of spices. Fresh fruit and vegetables from the Békaa Valley are also an important part of cooking. Many people shop at souks, which are open street markets. There shoppers find stalls and shops of fruits, vegetables, spices, meats, and other goods.

Food is essential to the Lebanese culture and visiting with one another. No matter the occasion, guests are offered coffee. Lebanese keep a variety of dishes on hand in the event of an unexpected guest. Basic dishes that store and reheat easily are staples in the Lebanese kitchen. It is also common to make dishes that can be used again to make other dishes, both for family meals and for unplanned guests.[2]

Mezze is an important part of Lebanese cuisine. "Mezze" comes from the Persian word "to taste." Today it means an array of small, hot and cold dishes set out on the table. Sometimes there can be up to 20 different items! Common mezze dishes include hummus, cheese, olives, vegetables, and *kibbeh* balls. **Kebobs** are often served for mezze too. They are pieces of meat and vegetables cooked on a skewer. Mezze is leisurely. People eat, drink, and talk for hours. Mezze even takes the place of a main meal sometimes. Dinner in Lebanon usually includes meat or fish. A grain dish is usually served, plus bread, a vegetable, a

IN CASE YOU WERE WONDERING

What do the Lebanese eat for dessert?
After a meal, diners cleanse their palate with fresh fruit or nuts. The Lebanese also enjoy sweet pastries.

This variety of foods served on small plates is an example of *mezze* in Lebanon.

salad, olives, and other items. Food is placed in the center of the table. Everyone serves themselves.[3]

While the Lebanese still eat much in the traditional way, there are many bars and restaurants. In the cities, people can visit restaurants that serve foods from around the world.

Holidays and Celebrations

Many holidays in Lebanon are celebrated by religion. Muslims observe **Ramadan**. During Ramadan, Muslims fast. That means they do not eat or drink during daylight hours. It is a holy period. During this time people think about whether they are living by Islamic teachings. They pray for forgiveness for sins. It is also a time for special prayers. At the end of Ramadan,

Lebanese orphans play traditional drums during a ceremony to celebrate the Muslim holy fasting month of Ramadan in Beirut.

Muslims enjoy a three day holiday called **Eid al-Fitr**. During this time, people feast with family and friends.[4]

For Christians, Easter and Christmas are important. In Lebanon, Christians celebrate these holidays much like they do in other parts of the world. Lebanese Christians decorate trees. They exchange gifts. Setting up a Nativity scene is important, too. The scene depicts the day Jesus was born. Most people go to midnight mass on December 24. On Easter, people take part in parades. They carry branches of palm leaves, flowers and candles. Holidays are always a time of celebrating with family.[5]

No matter the religion, everyone celebrates New Year's Day and Lebanon's Independence Day. Their Independence day is November 22. That is the day in 1943 on which Lebanon finally became its own country.

Lebanese youths release pigeons into the sky during a parade on Independence Day in Beirut.

Marriage

Getting married in Lebanon requires a marriage contract. The contract has to be signed by a member of a religious community. Couples must also list their religion and sect on the application. Most people do not marry someone from another sect. In the past, the only way that happened is if the woman converted to the man's religion. Up until 2013, Lebanon did not allow civil marriages, unions that were nonreligious, at all. This is because Lebanon is so divided by religion, and religious leaders control a lot of personal and political affairs. However, in 2013, one couple succeeded in having the first non-religious marriage.[6]

No matter the sect, or not, weddings follow Lebanese traditions. The most important is the **zaffeh**. This is when the bride is escorted to her husband. The bride's escort is made up of dancers and includes loud singing, drumming, and music. The tradition is very entertaining for guests. The wedding itself is grand. Friends and family attend in large numbers. The wedding reception includes food, dancing, and music that lasts all night long.

Traditional Lebanese weddings are known for their festive music and dancing led by a *zaffeh*.

GHADI—THE SECT-LESS BABY

Babies born in Lebanon are registered with the government. Parents must fill out a form. Part of it includes filling in the baby's sect, or religion. In September 2013, one set of parents left that section blank. The parents themselves have a civil marriage. So when their son, Ghadi, was born, they wanted to register him without a sect. He is the first sect-less baby to be born and legally registered in Lebanon.

The parents did it on purpose. They, and many others in Lebanon, are tired of religion determining everything in their country. People feel that officials run the country based on the needs of their sect. Instead, people like Ghadi's parents want the politicians to run the country based on what is best for Lebanon and all Lebanese people equally. Those who are opposed to the sectarianism applauded these parents' actions.

"When you remove the sect from your ID, you are taking a step forward toward a non-sectarian country where everyone has equal rights," said the mother. "I want my son to be a Lebanese citizen, not the son of a sect."

Yet not everyone approved. Many politicians and religious leaders have spoken against the steps towards dismantling the sectarian regime. One Sunni leader called the idea of civil marriages a "germ" in his society.

Nonetheless, Ghadi's parents hope that their actions will be the beginning of change. They want to stop giving power to the sectarian regime. They hope that Ghadi is the first of many sect-less babies who will grow up to be leaders of a non-sectarian Lebanon.[7]

Protesters carrying banners take part in a march against Lebanon's sectarian political system. People are tired of the stalemate in government and want politicians to focus on Lebanese citizens, no matter their religion.

A street vendor sells *darbukas*, traditional drums made of clay and goat skin.

CHAPTER 6
The Arts

Like everything else, the arts in Lebanon have been shaped by its heritage. Many crafts in Lebanon date back to the Phoenicians. Glass blowing came from ancient Egypt. During their trade and travel, the Phoenicians brought the art back to the region. They improved the craft. Soon their glass trade expanded around the world. The art of blown glass is still important in Lebanon today.

The same is true for metal working. Phoenician artifacts suggest they were masters at chiseling, engraving and decorating metal. The art evolved over time. Many glass and metal crafts are for sale today in Lebanon's souks. Vendors also sell ceramics, Arab-inspired jewelry, woven carpets, handmade baskets and much more. Each of these crafts were influenced by some part of Lebanon's past.

The Lebanese also applied their craftsmanship to making instruments. Using the famed cedars from the mountains of Lebanon, people carved wood. The **oud** is a stringed instrument made from wood. It is shaped like a pear. The oud is part of traditional music art in Lebanon. In this tradition, the oud musician plays alongside poets or singers.[1]

Another ancient instrument is the **darbuka** drum. It originated in the Middle East. The drum is made of clay with goat skin stretched across the top. It provides a relaxing and rhythmic beat in traditional Lebanese music. It is with this beat that the traditional folk dance, the **dabke**, is danced. Men and women hold hands and dance in a semi-circle. A Lebanese legend explains the origin of the dance. It began back in the days when people gathered to help friends build a new house. The tradition was that people would gather on the roof. Together they would help tamp down the mud and sticks. The dabke is still an important part of Lebanese dancing, especially in times of celebration.[2] Belly dancing is another popular form of dance. It is performed by women only. Dancers move their hips and bare stomachs to music. It began as a Middle Eastern folk dance. Back then the women danced alone or at parties or celebrations. Nowadays, the dance is much more common. The dancers wear sequined belts or bras that jangle when they move.[3]

Zajal folk poetry is another part of Lebanese heritage. It is improvised poetry, made up on the spot, and it is recited in a song. Some believe that *zajal* is a symbol of Lebanon's history. It reflects Lebanon's traditions, villages and history.[4]

There is modern music in Lebanon, too. The music scene in Beirut is lively. There are many different bands and singers who perform regularly. Young people also like to go to dance clubs. Radio stations play modern music. Some of the songs are from Lebanese musicians. Other music comes from around the world. Some young people have even turned to Arabic hip-hop. Young musicians gather on the streets. Without any instruments, they sing songs about their country, war and morality.[5]

The most famous of all Lebanese musicians is a woman named Fairuz. She sings about the Lebanese heritage and the

IN CASE YOU WERE WONDERING

What traditional games do the Lebanese play?

Backgammon, which is also popular in the West, is played in Lebanon. It is the world's oldest-known game and it originated in the Middle East region. Players move stones or markers on a board according to a roll of the dice.

country. The songs are poetic. Fairuz began singing as a young girl in the 1950s. By the 1970s she was a superstar in the current music scene. Since her rise to stardom she has traveled the world. Fairuz has performed from Brazil to the US. She even held record-breaking concerts at the Royal Festival Hall in London. She's become a symbol of the Lebanese people and a quest for peace in her country.[6]

Today Lebanon holds on to its many traditional arts, yet modern culture from around the world is evident. In Beirut, people can attend ballets, see the opera, and listen to symphonies. In addition, yearly festivals in other parts of Lebanon showcase both traditional and modern art.

Literature

Much of Lebanon's famous literature reflects its heritage. The literature of the 21st century often includes accounts of the country's brutal 15-year civil war. Authors write about growing up in a war zone and how it affected the Lebanese people. Books about the Middle East are gaining popularity in the West.

One writer, Elias Khoury, released a book in 2006 called *Gate of the Sun*. It tells the stories of the Palestinian refugee experience. Amid the hardships, Khoury tells stories of everyday life.[7] Another writer is award winning novelist, Alexandre Najjar. He has written historical novels and poems. He also published a biography about the famous Lebanese writer and philosopher, Kahlil Gibran. Najjar was born in 1967 and is considered one of the best writers of his generation.[8]

Recreation

What people do in their free time in Lebanon is partly affected by the climate. The temperatures are quite moderate and Lebanon gets about 300 sunny days a year! The water in the

Mediterranean is warm and clear. People enjoy fishing, swimming, snorkeling and boating off the coast of Lebanon. The weather there is hot and humid in the summer. Even in the winter, the temperatures are mild.

There are many places to go hiking in Lebanon's mountains in the spring, summer and fall. In the winter, snow covers the mountains. Many people drive from the cities to enjoy the snow. In fact, Lebanon is the only country in the Middle East where skiing is possible. It is an extremely popular sport in Lebanon. Yet, skiers can drive back to the coast to swim in the warm Mediterranean, all in one day! People in Lebanon also enjoy soccer (which they call football), basketball, volleyball, and other sports.[9]

Sports fields and parks are not common in Lebanon, but that doesn't stop children from playing "football" in an open, sandy lot.

KAHLIL GIBRAN

Kahlil Gibran is one of Lebanon's most famous people. He was born in 1883 in a small Lebanese village called Bsharri. At the age of twenty-three he published his first work, a collection of short stories. The focus of those stories, and his later work, was on spiritual questions. He believed that people should find a way to be in control

The Gibran Museum and Gibran's final resting place in Bsharri.

of their own lives. Also, Gibran called on sensible living and thinking. Gibran was influenced greatly by his mother. She had little education, however, she was wise. She spoke both Arabic and French fluently. Gibran's mother shared her musical and artistic talents with her son. She also told him Lebanese folktales and biblical stories. All of this fueled Gibran's already active imagination.

In 1895, Kahlil's mother and three siblings were forced to emigrate to the United States. For a while the young boy worked as a peddler on the streets of Boston. In 1898 he returned to Beirut for college. Gibran's most famous work, *The Prophet*, was published in 1923. It was an immediate success. It became a voice for those seeking peace. Gibran believed in bridging the gaps between all cultures, and ending human conflict. The book was translated into several languages. Gibran died in New York in 1931. He is buried in his home town of Bsharri.[10]

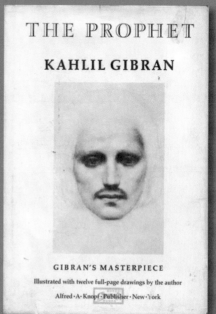

THE PROPHET

KAHLIL GIBRAN

GIBRAN'S MASTERPIECE
Illustrated with twelve full-page drawings by the author
Alfred·A·Knopf·Publisher·New·York

The Mohammad Al-Amin Mosque is a Sunni mosque located in Martyrs' Square in downtown Beirut, Lebanon. It was built between 2002 and 2007 by the former Lebanese Prime Minister Rafik Hariri. The statue commemorates Lebanese nationalists who were hanged during World War I by the Ottomans.

Women pray at Martyr Square during the Eid Al-Fitr in Tripoli, Lebanon.

traditional roles. What a woman wears also depends on her religion and where she lives in Lebanon. In the cities, such as Beirut, women dress much the same as they do in Western cities. Fashion is important in Lebanon. Some Muslim women, though, are required to be covered from head to toe. This is especially true for those living in rural areas. However, of all Arab countries, Lebanon is the least conservative. In Lebanon, many people are open to women not covering their heads in public. In other Arab countries, women are expected to cover at least their hair and ears.[9]

IN CASE YOU WERE WONDERING

What do the Lebanese watch on television?
The television stations air many of the same kinds of programs as those seen elsewhere in the world. Television listings include sitcoms, news stations, dramas, talk shows, sports, and more.

People enjoy the sand, sun, and the warm Mediterranean water along the coast in Beirut.

Conclusion

Lebanon is a nation of contrasts. It is a place where Western ideas intermingle with ancient tradition, where the cultures of thousands of years have left their footprint. Yet it is also a place where new footprints are welcomed, where old customs survive in the modern city of Beirut, and where Christians and Muslims coexist. They disagree, yet share a rich Arab culture.

Lebanon has experienced destruction and revival, domination and independence. Its outlook is progressive, yet traditional. Its people are strong and resilient, generous, and welcoming. But Lebanon is fragile. Peace is tenuous in this little country. War, sectarianism, and violence always seem to be just around the corner. The people, however, remain optimistic. They are, as they have always been, resilient.

FESTIVALS

The Lebanese are known around the world for their love of celebrating. It is not surprising, then, that the country has numerous festivals. Some of them even continue in the shadow of war.

The Beiteddine Festival in July and August attracts visitors from all over the Middle East. The festival includes both Lebanese and world famous artists. It takes place in a 200-year-old palace in the mountains of Lebanon. The first festival was held in 1985 during the civil war. The hope was to bring a sense of normalcy to the country. Founders wanted to highlight art in a time of war. More than 50,000 people attend every year. They are treated to a variety of performing arts, including dance, poetry, singing, music, and more. There are also exhibits at the Beiteddine Festival. Some artists display sculpture, photographs, and films. Despite the odds, the festival has grown every year.[10]

Another popular festival in Lebanon is the Baalbeck International Festival. It, too, is one of the most prestigious in the Middle East. It is the oldest festival in Lebanon. The festival was created in 1956 to promote the cultural and artistic aspects of Lebanon. The festival is also meant to bring in artists from other cultures. It takes place every year in the city of Baalbeck in the ancient ruins dating back to the Romans. From early July to the end of August, audiences enjoy performances from around the world. Shows include all kinds of music, dance, and plays.[11] In 2013, the war with Syria threatened the festival. But organizers did not cancel it. Instead, they moved it to a site near Beirut. The show must go on!

Dancers perform during the Beiteddine Art Festival in the 200-year-old palace. Each year the festival attracts tens of thousands of visitors.

HUMMUS

Hummus is a traditional mezze dish in Lebanon. It is made from chickpeas, a common ingredient in Lebanese cooking. Be sure to ask **an adult** before opening cans, running the blender, cooking the eggs or using a knife.

Ingredients

A 14 ounce can of chickpeas
   (also known as garbanzo
   beans)
1 teaspoon of crushed garlic
   (you can use pre-crushed
   garlic, or
   1-2 cloves of fresh garlic)
1 tablespoon tahini
1 tablespoon lemon juice
   (either straight from the
   lemon or bottled)
½ teaspoon salt
¼ teaspoon cumin
3 tablespoons olive oil
pita bread
olives from the
   Mediterranean region
4 hard-boiled eggs
2 tomatoes

Instructions

1. Drain and rinse the chickpeas. Put the chickpeas in a blender with the garlic, tahini, lemon juice, salt, cumin and olive oil.
2. Blend the ingredients. You may need to stop the blender and use a spatula to scrape the sides. Add a splash of olive oil if needed, but the mix should be paste-like.
3. Once the hummus is blended, scrape it out of the blender into a small serving bowl.
4. Cut the pita bread, tomatoes and hard boiled eggs into wedges; arrange on a plate with the hummus.
5. Serve and enjoy!

MOSAICS

The art of mosaics dates back thousands of years. People used bits of glass, shells, stones, and ceramics to create colorful decorations. Ancient mosaics can be found across what was once the Roman Empire, which at one time included parts of the Middle East. Across Lebanon, hundreds of mosaics from the Roman and other eras have survived through time. The images depict religious or mythological figures. Some create a scene. Other mosaics are simply colorful patterns.

Materials
Different colored
    construction paper
    (these will be the "bits"
    you use to create the
    mosaic)
Glue (glue sticks work
    best!)
A piece of blank paper

Directions
1. Look through books of mosaics to see some examples, or get online for ideas.
2. On the paper, print out a mosaic template or draw your own design.
3. Decide what colors you will use. Tear or cut the construction paper into bits, each one less than a square inch in size.
4. Glue the bits onto the paper according to your design.

WHAT YOU SHOULD KNOW ABOUT LEBANON

Official Country Name: Lebanese Republic
Capital: Beirut
Other Major Cities: Tripoli, Sidon, Tyre
Location: At the heart of the Middle East, bordered by the Mediterranean Sea to the west, Israel to the south, and Syria to the north and east
Land Area: 10,400 square km (6,464 square miles; smaller than the state of Connecticut)
Coastline: 225 km (140 miles)
Terrain: Narrow coastline, two mountain ranges and a fertile valley (it is the only country in the Middle East without a desert!)
Climate: Moderate; hot summers and cool, wet winters (the mountains receive enough snow for winter sports)
Major Resources: limestone, iron ore, salt, farmland
Government Type: Republic
National Symbol: Cedar tree
Official Language: Arabic
Population: 5,882,562 (July 2014 estimate)
Ethnic Groups: Arab 95%, Armenian 4%, other 1%
Religions: Muslim 54% (27% Sunni, 27% Shiite); Christian 40.5% (includes 21% Maronite Catholic, 8% Greek Orthodox, 5% Greek Catholic, 6.5% other Christian); Druze 5.6%; very small numbers of Jews, Baha'is, Buddhists, Hindus, and Mormons
Literacy Rate: 89.6%

FLAG: The Lebanese flag was adopted on December 7, 1943 after gaining independence on November 22, 1943. The red stripes symbolize the blood shed for independence; the white band stands for peace and the snow on Lebanon's mountains. The tree in the center of the flag is a cedar tree, representing eternity, stability, happiness, and wealth.

TIMELINE

BCE

7500   Settlers establish the first villages in the region.

3500   Phoenician civilization grows and thrives; they establish trading centers and ports on the coast.

800   Phoenician prosperity and autonomy declines as the Assyrian empire gains power.

64   Romans invade and control the area for 600 years. Christianity develops under Roman rule.

CE

395   Byzantine Empire takes control of the region.

637   Arabs conquer Lebanon.

1095–1291   The Crusaders attempt to regain control of the region and reinstate Christianity.

1291–1516   Mamelouks drive out the Crusaders; they develop the commercial ports in Beirut.

1516–1918   Ottoman rule over the Middle East; Lebanon experiences some autonomy during this time.

1920   Lebanon comes under French control.

1926   The Lebanese constitution is written, using the French one as a model

1943   Lebanon Republic becomes an independent country, beginning twenty years of great prosperity for Lebanon.

1948   The country of Israel is formed, beginning a wave of Palestinian refugees into Lebanon.

1975–1989   Devastating civil war in Lebanon; during this time Syrian and Israeli troops enter Lebanon.

1982   International peace-keeping forces enter Lebanon.

1983   The US Embassy and Marine barracks in Beirut are bombed, killing over 200 Marines.

1985   International peace-keepers leave because of excessive violence

1989   The Ta'if Agreements are signed; in part they redistribute political power among the various religious sects.

1992   Rafik Hariri is elected Prime Minister, and is credited with beginning the reconstruction of Lebanon.

2000   Israel finally withdraws its troops from Lebanon.

2005   Prime Minister Rafik Hariri is killed by a truck bomb along with twenty-two others. Syria withdraws troops from Lebanon after more than thirty years.

2006   Israeli and Hezbollah forces clash in Lebanon.

2011   Lebanon's neighbor, Syria, falls into civil war, igniting existing tensions between Muslim groups.

2013   Conflict on the Lebanese/Syrian border increases, with violence often erupting in northern Lebanon; Syrian refugees flood into the country.

2014   As of June, 2,500 new Syrian refugees arrive in Lebanon daily; more than half are children.

CHAPTER NOTES

Introduction

1. Lebanon Ministry of Tourism, "Profile of Lebanon" http://www.destinationlebanon.gov.lb/en/DiscoverLebanon/details/1

Chapter 1. Living in Lebanon

1. The World Bank, "Lebanon: Greater Beirut Water Supply Project" http://web.worldbank.org/WBSITE/EXTERNAL/COUNTRIES/MENAEXT/LEBANONEXTN/0,,contentMDK:22792108~pagePK:1497618~piPK:217854~theSitePK:294904,00.html

2. *Beirut* (Pilot Productions, 2007)

3. Peter Chaalan (Lebanese citizen), personal interview with the author, January 10 2014.

4. Ibid.

5. Suad Amari. *Cooking the Lebanese Way* (Minneapolis: Lerner Publications Company, 1986), pp. 16–19.

6. Peter Chaalan (Lebanese citizen), personal interview with the author, January 10 2014.

7. Lebanon Ministry of Tourism, "Lebanon—A Heaven on Earth" http://www.mot.gov.lb/Content/uploads/Publication/1210180127 27087~Brochure.pdf

8. Lebanon Ministry of Tourism, "Profile of Lebanon" http://www.destinationlebanon.gov.lb/en/DiscoverLebanon/details/1

9. Lebanon Ministry of Tourism, "Discover Lebanon" http://www.destinationlebanon.gov.lb/

Chapter 2. History

1. Lebanese Global Information Center, "Phoenicians" http://www.lgic.org/en/phoenicians.php

2. Lebanon Ministry of Tourism, "Discover Lebanon" http://www.destinationlebanon.gov.lb/en/DiscoverLebanon

3. The National Museum of Beirut, "The Iron Age" http://www.beirutnationalmuseum.com/e-collection-fer.htm

4. Lebanon Ministry of Tourism, "Quick Facts" http://www.destinationlebanon.gov.lb/en/DiscoverLebanon/details/1/5

5. Ibid.

6. BBC News Middle East, "Lebanon Profile" http://www.bbc.co.uk/news/world-middle-east-14647308

7. Lebanon Ministry of Tourism, "Quick Facts" http://www.destinationlebanon.gov.lb/en/DiscoverLebanon/details/1/5

8. BBC News Middle East, "Lebanon Profile" http://www.bbc.co.uk/news/world-middle-east-14649284

9. Lebanon Ministry of Tourism, "Quick Facts" http://www.destinationlebanon.gov.lb/en/DiscoverLebanon/details/1/5

10. BBC News Middle East, "Lebanon Profile" http://www.bbc.co.uk/news/world-middleeast-14649284

11. Joshua Hammer, "Precarious Lebanon" http://www.smithsonianmag.com/people-places/precarious-lebanon.html

12. *Lebanon—A Heaven on Earth* (Beirut: Lebanon Ministry of Tourism, nd) http://www.mot.gov.lb/Content/uploads/Publication/1210180 12727087~Brochure.pdf

13. Hassan Salameh Sarkis, *Anjar* (Beirut: Lebanon Ministry of Tourism, nd) http://mot.gov.lb/Content/uploads/Publication/12080602450 9919~Anjar%20English.pdf

14. Elain Larwood, Marilyn Raschka and Dr.Hassan Salameh Sarkis, *Tyr* (Beirut: Lebanon Ministry of Tourism, nd) http://mot.gov.lb/Content/uploads/Publication/120806041438669~TYR%20%20ENG.pdf

15. Beiteddine Art Festival 2013, "Beiteddine Palace History" http://beiteddine.org/#palace

16. Hassan Salameh Sarkis, *Tripoli* (Beirut: Lebanon Ministry of Tourism, nd) http://mot.gov.lb/Content/uploads/Publication/12080604122 9060~TRIPOLI%20ENG.pdf

Chapter 3. Cultures

1. Lebanon Ministry of Tourism, "Quick Facts" http://www.destinationlebanon.gov.lb/en/DiscoverLebanon/details/1/5

2. Beirut National Museum, "From the Arab Conquest to the Mamluk Period" http://www.beirutnationalmuseum.com/e-collection-arabe.htm

3. Maronite Heritage, "History of the Maronites" http://www.maronite-heritage.com/LNE.php?page=History

4. CIA, "Lebanon" https://www.cia.gov/library/publications/the-world-factbook/geos/le.html

5. CIA, "Lebanon" https://www.cia.gov/library/publications/the-world-factbook/geos/le.html

6. Samuel Helfont, "Th e Geopolitics of the Sunni-Shi'i Divide in the Middle East" http://www.fpri.org/articles/2013/12/geopolitics-sunni-shii-divide-middle-east

7. PBS Frontline, "Lebanon—Party of God" http://www.pbs.org/frontlineworld/stories/lebanon/thestory.html

8. Jonathan Master and Zachary Laub. "Hezbollah (a.k.a. Hizbollah, Hizbu'llah)" http://www.cfr.org/lebanon/hezbollah-k-hizbollah-hizbullah/p9155

9. *Exile Without End—Palestinians In Lebanon* (CBC Radio-Canada, nd) http://www.cbc.ca/news2/interactives/shatila/

10. Ibid.

11. Lebanon Ministry of Tourism, "Quick Facts" http://www.destinationlebanon.gov.lb/en/DiscoverLebanon/details/1/5

12. Josh Wood, "Palestinians Long Wait in Lebanon" http://www.nytimes.com/2011/03/03/world/middleeast/03iht-m03-lebanon.html?_r=0

CHAPTER NOTES

13: *Exile Without End—Palestinians in Lebanon* (CBC Radio-Canada, nd) http://www.cbc.ca/new2/interactives/shatila/

Chapter 4. Current Issues

1. Peter Chaalan (Lebanese citizen), personal interview with the author, January 10 2014.
2. Aljazeera, "Lebanese Government Collapses" http://www.aljazeera.com/news/middleeast/2011/01/2011112151356430829.html
3. The World Bank, "Water in Lebanon: Matching Myth with Reality" http://www.worldbank.org/en/news/feature/2013/12/23/water-in-lebanon-matching-myth-with-reality
4. Mohamed Azakir, "Bomb blast in Beirut kills prominent politician" http://america.aljazeera.com/articles/2013/12/27/bomb-blast-in-beirutkillsseveralincludingprominentpolitician.html
5. Aryn Baker, "Lebanon May Become 'Center' of Arab World's Sectarian Wars" http://world.time.com/2014/01/16/lebanon-hariri-sectarian-arab-wars/
6. *Can Tenuous Peace Among Lebanon's Religious Sects Survive Stress of Syria's War?* (PBS Newshour, June 7, 2013) http://www.pbs.org/newshour/bb/world/jan-june13/
7. Lebanon Ministry of Tourism, "Quick Facts" http://www.destinationlebanon.gov.lb/en/DiscoverLebanon/details/1/5
8. Mounira Chaieb, "Young in the Arab World: Lebanon" http://news.bbc.co.uk/2/hi/middle_east/4212973.stm
9. Central Administration of Statistics, "About Lebanon" http://www.cas.gov.lb/index.php/en/about-lebanon-en
10. Aljazeera, "Fanning Lebanon's sectarian flames?" http://www.aljazeera.com/programmes/insidestory/2014/01/fanning-lebanon-sectarian-flames-20141177281161970.html

Chapter 5. Family

1. Peter Chaalan (Lebanese citizen), personal interview with the author, January 10 2014.
2. Dawn, Elaine and Selwa Anthony. *Lebanese Cooking.* North Clarendon, VT: Periplus Editions, Ltd., 2005. Print. 10-12.
3. Dawn, Elaine and Selwa Anthony. *Lebanese Cooking.* North Clarendon, VT: Periplus Editions, Ltd., 2005. Print. 10.
4. Mark Tibbits, "The Islamic Holy Month of Ramadan in 2011, 2012, 2013" https://suite101.com/a/the-islamic-holy-month-of-ramadan-in-2011-2012-2013-a352306
5. BBC News, "Christmas in Lebanon" http://news.bbc.co.uk/dna/place-lancashire/plain/A10451206
6. Dalal Mawad. "Lebanon civil marriage raises hope for change" http://www.aljazeera.com/indepth/features/2013/04/20134309242619227.html

7. Michel Pizzi, "Lebanese couple announces country's first 'sect-less' baby" http://america.aljazeera.com/articles/2013/11/1/lebanon-s-first-sectlessbaby.html

Chapter 6. The Arts

1. Lebanon Ministry of Tourism, "Handicraft" http://www.destinationlebanon.gov.lb/en/DiscoverLebanon/details/2/10
2. World Lebanese Cultural Union, "The Origin of the Lebanese Dabke" http://www.ulcm.org/culture/traditions/lebanese-dabke
3. *Beirut* (Pilot Productions, 2007).
4. http://www.aljazeera.com/programmes/nextmusicstation/2011/05/201151211634617569.html
5. *Beirut* (Pilot Productions, 2007).
6. Fairuz Online, "Biography" http://fairuzonline.com/alegend.htm
7. Lorraine Adams, "Palestinian Lives" http://www.nytimes.com/2006/01/15/books/review/15adams.html
8. Alexandre Najjar, "Home" http://www.najjar.org/en/index.asp
9. Lebanon Ministry of Tourism, "Quick Facts" http://www.destinationlebanon.gov.lb/en/DiscoverLebanon/details/1/5
10. Kahlil Gibran, "Biography" http://www.gibrankhalilgibran.org/pages.php?mvkey=4

Chapter 7. Lebanon Today

1. Lebanon Ministry of Tourism, "Quick Facts" http://www.destinationlebanon.gov.lb/en/DiscoverLebanon/details/1/5
2. BBC News Middle East, "Lebanon Profile" http://www.bbc.co.uk/news/world-middle-east-14648683
3. CIA, "Lebanon" https://www.cia.gov/library/publications/the-world-factbook/geos/le.html
4. Ibid.
5. Lebanon Ministry of Tourism, "Discover Lebanon" http://www.destinationlebanon.gov.lb/en/DiscoverLebanon
6. Elain Larwood, Marilyn Raschka and Dr.Hassan Salameh Sarkis, *Tyr* (Beirut: Lebanon Ministry of Tourism, nd) http://mot.gov.lb/Content/uploads/Publication/120806041438669~TYR%20%20ENG.pdf
7. Hassan Salameh Sarkis, *Tripoli* (Beirut: Lebanon Ministry of Tourism, nd) http://mot.gov.lb/Content/uploads/Publication/120806041229060~TRIPOLI%20ENG.pdf
8. *Beirut* (Pilot Productions, 2007).
9. Ibid.
10. Beiteddine Art Festival 2013, "Beiteddine Art Festival—Story" http://beiteddine.org/#art_festival
11. Baalbeck International Festival, "History" http://www.baalbeck.org.lb/index.php/en/the-festival/lang-enhistorylanglang-frhistoirelang

FURTHER READING

Books

Anthony, Dawn, Elaine and Selwa. *Lebanese Cooking*. North Clarendon, Vermont: Periplus Editions, Ltd., 2005.

Aretha, David. *Lebanon in the News—Past, Present and Future*. Berkeley Heights, New Jersey: Enslow Publishers, Inc., 2006.

Sheehan, Sean and Zawiah Abdul Latif. *Cultures of the World—Lebanon*. New York: Marshall Cavendish Benchmark, 2007.

Willis, Terri. *Lebanon—Enchantment of the World*. New York: Scholastic, 2005.

On the Internet

The Embassy of Lebanon—Washington, DC: *The Country of Lebanon*. http://www.lebanonembassyus.org/the-country-of-lebanon.html

Lebanon Ministry of Tourism: *Only Lebanon,* "Discover Lebanon." http://www.destinationlebanon.gov.lb/en/DiscoverLebanon

The World Bank: *Lebanon.* http://web.worldbank.org/WBSITE/EXTERNAL/COUNTRIES/MENAEXT/LEBANONEXTN/0,,menuPK:294909~pagePK:141159~piPK:141110~theSitePK:294904,00.html

Central Intelligence Agency: T*he World Factbook,* "Lebanon." https://www.cia.gov/library/publications/the-world-factbook/geos/le.html

Works Consulted

Alexandre Najjar: *Home* (accessed January 25, 2014) http://www.najjar.org/en/index.asp

Amari, Suad. *Cooking the Lebanese Way*. Minneapolis: Lerner Publications Company, 1986. Print.

Anthony, Dawn, Elaine and Selwa. *Lebanese Cooking*. North Clarendon, VT: Periplus Editions, Ltd., 2005. Print.

Azakir, Mohamed. "Bomb blast in Beirut kills prominent politician." *Aljazeera America,* December 27, 2013 (accessed January 20, 2014) http://america.aljazeera.com/articles/2013/12/27/bomb-blast-in-beirutkillsseveralincludingprominentpolitician.html

Baalbeck International Festival: *The Festival,* "History" (accessed January 25, 2104) http://www.baalbeck.org.lb/index.php/en/the-festival/lang-enhistorylanglang-frhistoirelang

Beiteddine Art Festival 2013: *Beiteddine Palace,* "History" (accessed January 6, 2014) http://beiteddine.org/#palace

Beirut. Narrated by Merriless Parker. Pilot Productions, 2007. DVD.

Can Tenuous Peace Among Lebanon's Religious Sects Survive Stress of Syria's War? Reported by Margaret Warner. PBS Newshour, June 7, 2013. Online newscast. http://www.pbs.org/newshour/bb/world-jan-june13-lebanon_06-07/

Central Administration of Statistics: *About Lebanon* (accessed January 11, 2014) http://www.cas.gov.lb/index.php/en/about-lebanon-en

Central Intelligence Agency: *The World Factbook,* "Lebanon" (accessed January 5, 2014) https://www.cia.gov/library/publications/the-world-factbook/geos/le.html

Baker, Aryn. "Lebanon May Become 'Center' of Arab World's Sectarian Wars." *TIME—World,* January 16, 2014. http://world.time.com/2014/01/16/lebanon-hariri-sectarian-arab-wars/

Chaieb, Mounira. "Young in the Arab World: Lebanon." B*BC News Middle East,* February 8, 2005 (accessed January 10, 2014) http://news.bbc.co.uk/2/hi/middle_east/4212973.stm

"Christmas in Lebanon." *BBC News,* nd (accessed January 29, 2014) http://news.bbc.co.uk/dna/place-lancashire/plain/A10451206

Destination The Middle East. Narrated by Ian Wright. Escapi, 2003. DVD.

The Embassy of Lebanon—Washington, DC: *The Country of Lebanon* (accessed January 2, 2014) http://www.lebanonembassyus.org/the-country-of-lebanon.html

Exile Without End—Palestinians In Lebanon. Reported by Nahlah Ayed, Ahmed Kouaou and Danny Braün. CBC Radio-Canada, nd. Online documentary. http://www.cbc.ca/news2/interactives/shatila/

Fairuz Online: *A Legend,* "Biography" (accessed January 25, 2014) http://fairuzonline.com/alegend.htm

"Fanning Lebanon's sectarian flames?" *Aljazeera,* January 17, 2014 (accessed January 25, 2014) http://www.aljazeera.com/programmes/insidestory/2014/01/fanning-lebanon-sectarian-flames-20141177281161970.html

Hammer, Joshua. "Precarious Lebanon." *Smithsonian Magazine,* July 2008. http://www.smithsonianmag.com/history/precarious-lebanon-8822/

Helfont, Samuel. *Foreign Policy Research Institute,* "The Geopolitics of the Sunni-Shi'i Divide in the Middle East," December 2013 (accessed January 22, 2014) http://www.fpri.org/articles/2013/12/geopolitics-sunni-shii-divide-middle-east

Kahlil Gibran: *About Gibran,* "Biography" (accessed January 25, 2014) http://www.gibrankhalilgibran.org/pages.php?mvkey=4

FURTHER READING

Khayat, Marie Karam and Margaret Clark Keatinge. *Lebanon—Land of the Cedars*. Beirut: Khayat Book and Publishing Company, 1967. Print.

Lebanon Ministry of Tourism: *Only Lebanon*, "Discover Lebanon" (accessed January 2, 2014) http://www.destinationlebanon.gov.lb/en/DiscoverLebanon

Lebanese Books, Inc.: *Kids Books in English* (accessed January 25, 2014) http://www.lebanesebooks.com/Merchant2/merchant.mvc?Screen=CTGY&Category_Code=Kids_eng

Lebanese Broadcasting Corporation International: *Shows* (accessed January 25, 2014) http://www.lbcgroup.tv/shows/en

Lebanese Global Information Center: *The Ancient People of Lebanon*, "Phoenicians" (accessed January 22, 2014) http://www.lgic.org/en/phoenicians.php

Liban Mall: *Weddings*, "Zaffe in Lebanon" http://www.lebanesemall.com/b2b/template-client.php?clientid=939&subid=26

Larwood, Elaine, Marilyn Raschka and Dr. Hassan Salameh Sarkis. Tyr. *Beirut: Lebanon Ministry of Tourism*, nd. Online brochure. http://mot.gov.lb/Content/uploads/Publication/120806041438669~TYR%20%20ENG.pdf

Lebanon—A Heaven on Earth. Beirut: Lebanon Ministry of Tourism, nd. Online brochure. http://www.mot.gov.lb/Content/uploads/Publication/12101801272 7087~Brochure.pdf

Lebanon—Party of God. Reported by David Lewis. PBS Frontline, May 2003. Online video. http://www.pbs.org/frontlineworld/stories/lebanon/thestory.html

"Lebanon Profile." *BBC News Middle East*, December 31 2013 (accessed January 7, 2014) http://www.bbc.co.uk/news/world-middle-east-14649284

"Lebanese Government Collapses." *Aljazeera*, January 13, 2011 (accessed January 23, 2014) http://www.aljazeera.com/news/middleeast/2011/01/2011112151356430829.html

Maronite Heritage: *History of the Maronites* (accessed January 6, 2014) http://www.maronite-heritage.com/LNE.php?page=History

Master, Jonathan and Zachary Laub. *Council on Foreign Relations*, "Hezbollah (a.k.a. Hizbollah, Hizbu'llah)", January 3, 2014 (accessed January 10, 2014) http://www.cfr.org/lebanon/hezbollah-k-hizbollah-hizbullah/p9155

Mawad, Dalal. "Lebanon civil marriage raises hope for change." *Aljazeera*, May 2, 2013 (accessed January 15, 2014) http://www.aljazeera.com/indepth/features/2013/04/20134309242619227.html

The National Museum of Beirut: *Collections* (accessed January 3, 2014) http://beirutnationalmuseum.com/e-collections.htm

Pizzi, Michel. "Lebanese couple announces country's first 'sect-less' baby." *Aljazeera America*, November 1, 2013 (accessed January 15, 2014) http://america.aljazeera.com/articles/2013/11/1/lebanon-s-first-sectlessbaby.html

Poushter, Jacob. *Pew Research Center*, "How people in Muslim countries prefer women to dress in public," January 8, 2014 (accessed January 25, 2014). http://www.pewresearch.org/fact-tank/2014/01/08/what-is-appropriate-attire-for-women-in-muslim-countries/

Sarkis, Hassan Salameh. *Anjar*. Beirut: Lebanon Ministry of Tourism, nd. Online brochure. http://mot.gov.lb/Content/uploads/Publication/120806024509919~Anjar%20English.pdf

Sarkis, Hassan Salameh. *Baalbeck*. Beirut: Lebanon Ministry of Tourism, nd. Online brochure. http://mot.gov.lb/Content/uploads/Publication/120806024713138~Baalbeck%20English.pdf

Sarkis, Hassan Salameh. *Tripoli*. Beirut: Lebanon Ministry of Tourism, nd. Online brochure. http://mot.gov.lb/Content/uploads/Publication/120806041229060~TRIPOLI%20ENG.pdf

Tibbits, Mark. *Suite101*, "The Islamic Holy Month of Ramadan in 2011, 2012, 2013" (accessed January 15, 2014) https://suite101.com/a/the-islamic-holy-month-of-ramadan-in-2011-2012-2013-a352306

Vance, Peggy and Celia Goodrick-Clark. *The Mosaic Book—Ideas, Projects and Techniques*. North Pomfret, VT: Trafalgar Square Publishing. 1996. Print.

Wood, Josh. "Palestinians Long Wait in Lebanon." *The New York Times—Middle East*. 2 March 2011. http://www.nytimes.com/2011/03/03/world/middleeast/03iht-m03-lebanon.html?_r=0

The World Bank: *News*, "Water in Lebanon: Matching Myth with Reality," December 23, 2103 (accessed January 25, 2014) http://www.worldbank.org/en/news/feature/2013/12/23/water-in-lebanon-matching-myth-with-reality

The World Bank: *Lebanon*, "Lebanon: Greater Beirut Water Supply Project" (accessed January 5, 2014) http://web.worldbank.org/WBSITE/EXTERNAL/COUNTRIES/MENAEXT/LEBANONEXTN/0,,menuPK:294909~pagePK:141159~piPK:141110~theSitePK:294904,00.html

World Lebanese Cultural Union: *Culture*, "The Origin of the Lebanese Dabke" (accessed 15 January 2014) http://www.ulcm.org/culture/traditions/lebanese-dabke

GLOSSARY

Arabs—Descendants of people from the Arabian Peninsula.

dabke (deb-KUH)—A traditional folk dance.

darbuka (dar-BOO-ka)—A drum made of clay with goat skin stretched across the top.

democracy (deh-MOK-ruh-see)—A form of government in which the people elect their leaders.

domesticate (doh-MES-ti-kayt)—Tame, train and breed animals.

Eid al-Fitr (EED-al-fitter)—The festival marking the end of Ramadan; it is a time of celebrating and feasting and celebration with family and friends.

entrepreneurial (ahn-truh-pruh-NUR-ee-al)—Creative in business.

falafel (fuh-la-fel)—A meal of mashed chickpeas formed into balls and fried.

infrastructure (IN-fruh-struhk-cher)—The basic facilities of a society, such as power, water and roads.

Islam (IZ-lam)—The religion of Muslims who follow the teachings of Muhammad.

kebobs (keh-bobs)—Pieces of meat and vegetables cooked on a skewer.

kibbeh (KI-beh)—A favorite food in Lebanon made of lamb ground into a paste and seasoned with spices.

manouché (man-OU-shay)—An Arab-style bread common in Lebanon.

meghli (meg-HUH-lee)—A sweet rice pudding traditionally served to guests visiting a new baby.

mezze (me-ZAY)—An array of small, hot and cold dishes set out on the table.

Muslim—One who follows the religion of Islam.

oud (ood)—A pear-shaped stringed instrument.

parliamentary system—A system of government in which executive power lies with the legislature.

patriarch (PAY-tree-ahrk)—The male head of a family.

Phoenicians (fih-NEE-shuhns)—Some of the earliest inhabitants of the Lebanon region; they were skilled seaman, traders, and artisans.

Ramadan (RAH-meh-dahn)—A holy period in the Islamic religion during which Muslims do not eat or drink during daylight hours.

refugee (rehf-yoo-GEE)—Someone who is forced to leave their country due to war, persecution, or natural disasters.

sect (SEKT)—A group of people with different religious beliefs than others in a larger group to which they belong.

sectarian (sek-TAIR-ee-uhn)—Having to do with sects.

souk (sook)—An open market with vendors selling all types of food and crafts.

Westernized (WES-ter-nahyzed)—DEFINITION

zaatar (ZA-tar)—A blend of spices used in cooking.

zaffeh (ZA-fay)—This is when a bride is escorted to her husband accompanied by dancers, loud singing, drumming, and music.

Zajal—A traditional form of folk poetry recited in song; the poems are made up on the spot.

INDEX

About the Author

Laura Perdew is a mom, author, and former middle school teacher. She writes books for the education market, novels, and travel guides. Laura was born in Beirut, Lebanon. She has always enjoyed the stories her parents tell of living in Beirut during its time of prosperity, before the civil war. One day Laura hopes to be able to travel there. Now she can be found running, hiking, camping, and playing with her twin boys and husband in Boulder, Colorado.

LEBANON

North of Beirut is Lebanon's second largest city, Tripoli. It is famous for its **falafel** and busy souks. Falafel is made of ground chickpeas and spices. This mixture is formed into balls. The falafel is then fried. It is usually eaten on bread with tomatoes, tahini, and mint. Tripoli is famous for its architecture. The style was influenced by the Christian Crusades and the Ottoman rule. Many medieval buildings from the 14th century still stand in the port area. The other, modern part of the city is the business center. Today it is lively and thriving. However, the conflict in Syria has brought violence into Tripoli. It has also worsened the sectarian tensions in that city.[7]

Some Lebanese live in rural areas of the country. In fact, nomadic gypsies still live in the hills above Tripoli! They move

Tripoli today is a vibrant, modern city. It got its name, which means "tri-city," because in ancient times it was three cities in one.

with their herds of goats, and collect wild herbs to cook with. They live in tents and cook over open fires, much the same as their ancestors have done for centuries. Other people live in small villages scattered across Lebanon. Life there follows more traditional customs. Many of them are farmers. There are also many vineyards in the Békaa valley.[8]

Women in Lebanon

Women living in Lebanon have a more progressive life than in other Arab countries. Lebanon has even been considered a leader in the region for women's rights. To begin, women in Lebanon have equal civil rights to men. This is written in the constitution. They can vote, own businesses, and travel without a husband's permission. Girls go to school alongside boys. Many girls go to college. And even in the family, women often work outside the home. Even some of the positions in the National Assembly are held by women.

Still, Lebanon remains a patriarchal society. That means it is controlled by males. There are still many traditional gender roles in Lebanon. For example, women are still responsible for caring for the home, even if they have another job. Further, women who marry a man from another country cannot pass her nationality on to her children.

The role a woman has in Lebanon partly depends on her religion. Conservative Muslims require women to follow more

IN CASE YOU WERE WONDERING

Is there a difference between an Arab and a Muslim?

The word 'Arab' refers to one's ethnicity. Arabs are descendants of people from the Arabian Peninsula. They migrated and inhabited the Middle East and North Africa. The word 'Muslim' refers to one's religion. Today in the Arab world the main religion is Islam. These people are Muslims. Therefore, there are both Arab Muslims and Arab Christians in the Middle East.